I0413241

Quality-Assurance Data for Routine Water Analyses by the U.S. Geological Survey Laboratory in Troy, New York— July 2001 through June 2003

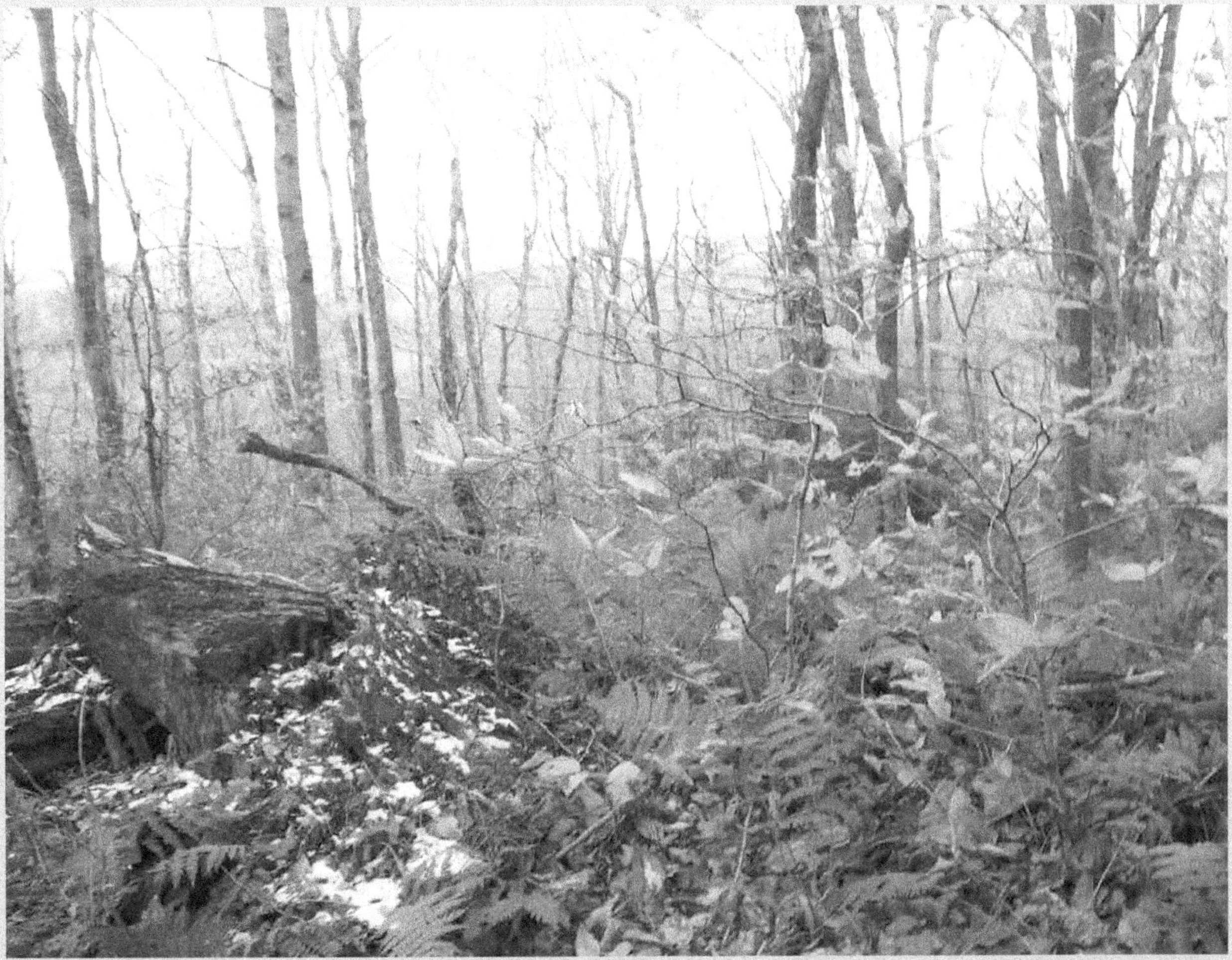

Open-File Report 2009–1232

U.S. Department of the Interior
U.S. Geological Survey

Cover. Late October view showing ferns, beech, other hardwood-conifer, and snow along the Wittenberg-Cornell-Slide Trail to Wittenberg Mountain in Catskill State Park, New York City Watershed, Ulster County, New York ©2006 Amanda Bailey

Quality-Assurance Data for Routine Water Analyses by the U.S. Geological Survey Laboratory in Troy, New York— July 2001 Through June 2003

By Tricia A. Lincoln, Debra A. Horan-Ross, Michael R. McHale, and Gregory B. Lawrence

Open-File Report 2009–1232

U.S. Department of the Interior
U.S. Geological Survey

U.S. Department of the Interior
KEN SALAZAR, Secretary

U.S. Geological Survey
Marcia K. McNutt, Director

U.S. Geological Survey, Reston, Virginia 2009

For more information on the USGS—the Federal source for science about the Earth,
its natural and living resources, natural hazards, and the environment:
World Wide Web: http://www.usgs.gov
Telephone: 1-888-ASK-USGS

Any use of trade, product, or firm names is for descriptive purposes only and does not imply
endorsement by the U.S. Government.

Although this report is in the public domain, permission must be secured from the individual
copyright owners to reproduce any copyrighted material contained within this report.

Suggested citation:
Lincoln, T.A., Horan-Ross, D.A., McHale, M.R., and Lawrence, G.B., 2009, Quality-assurance data for routine
water analyses by the U.S. Geological Survey laboratory in Troy, New York—July 2001 through June 2003:
U.S. Geological Survey Open-File Report 2009–1232, 32 p., available only at http://pubs.usgs.gov/of/2009/1232/.

Contents

Figures

Tables

Conversion Factors and Abbreviations

Multiply	By	To obtain
	Length	
centimeter (cm)	0.3937	inch (in.)
	Volume	
liter (L)	33.82	ounce, fluid (fl. oz)

Abbreviated Units of Measurement

mq/L   milligrams per liter
µeq/L   microequivalents per liter
µmol/L   micromoles per liter
µS/cm   microsiemens per centimeter
µg/L   micrograms per liter

Other Abbreviations

ANC   Acid-neutralizing capacity
AV   Analyzed value
CV   Coefficient of variation
D   Percent Difference
DI   Deionized Water
DOC   Dissolved organic carbon
DQO   Data-quality objective
MCV   Mean concentration value
MPV   Most probable value
NWRI   National Water Research Institute
QA   Quality assurance
QC   Quality Control
QC-high   High-concentration quality-control sample
QC-low   Low-concentration quality-control sample
SRS   Standard Reference Sample
TV   Troy Laboratory value
USGS   U.S. Geological Survey

Quality-Assurance Data for Routine Water Analyses by the U.S. Geological Survey Laboratory in Troy, New York— July 2001 Through June 2003

By Tricia A. Lincoln, Debra A. Horan-Ross, Michael R. McHale, and Gregory B. Lawrence

Abstract

The laboratory for analysis of low-ionic-strength water at the U.S. Geological Survey (USGS) Water Science Center in Troy, N.Y., analyzes samples collected by USGS projects throughout the Northeast. The laboratory's quality-assurance program is based on internal and interlaboratory quality-assurance samples and quality-control procedures that were developed to ensure proper sample collection, processing, and analysis. The quality-assurance and quality-control data were stored in the laboratory's Lab Master data-management system, which provides efficient review, compilation, and plotting of data. This report presents and discusses results of quality-assurance and quality control samples analyzed from July 2001 through June 2003.

Results for the quality-control samples for 19 analytical procedures were evaluated for bias and precision. Control charts indicate that data for six of the analytical procedures were occasionally biased for either high-concentration or low-concentration samples but were within control limits; these procedures were: acid-neutralizing capacity, chloride, magnesium, nitrate (ion chromatography), potassium, and sodium. The calcium procedure was biased throughout the analysis period for the high-concentration sample, but was within control limits. The total monomeric aluminum and fluoride procedures were biased throughout the analysis period for the low-concentration sample, but were within control limits. The total aluminum, pH, specific conductance, and sulfate procedures were biased for the high-concentration and low-concentration samples, but were within control limits.

Results from the filter-blank and analytical-blank analyses indicate that the procedures for 16 of 18 analytes were within control limits, although the concentrations for blanks were occasionally outside the control limits. The data-quality objective was not met for the dissolved organic carbon or specific conductance procedures.

Sampling and analysis precision are evaluated herein in terms of the coefficient of variation obtained for triplicate samples in the procedures for 18 of the 21 analytes. At least 90 percent of the samples met data-quality objectives for all procedures except total monomeric aluminum (83 percent of samples met objectives), total aluminum (76 percent of samples met objectives), ammonium (73 percent of samples met objectives), dissolved organic carbon (86 percent of samples met objectives), and nitrate (81 percent of samples met objectives). The data-quality objective was not met for the nitrite procedure.

Results of the USGS interlaboratory Standard Reference Sample (SRS) Project indicated satisfactory or above data quality over the time period, with most performance ratings for each sample in the good-to-excellent range. The N-sample (nutrient constituents) analysis had one unsatisfactory rating for the ammonium procedure in one study. The T-sample (trace constituents) analysis had one unsatisfactory rating for the magnesium procedure and one marginal rating for the potassium procedure in one study and one unsatisfactory rating for the sodium procedure in another.

Results of Environment Canada's National Water Research Institute (NWRI) program indicated that at least 90 percent of the samples met data-quality objectives for 10 of the 14 analytes; the exceptions were acid-neutralizing capacity, ammonium, dissolved organic carbon, and sodium. Data-quality objectives were not met in 37 percent of samples analyzed for acid-neutralizing capacity, 28 percent of samples analyzed for dissolved organic carbon, and 30 percent of samples analyzed for sodium. Results indicate a positive bias for the ammonium procedure in one study and a negative bias in another.

Results from blind reference-sample analyses indicated that data-quality objectives were met by at least 90 percent of the samples analyzed for calcium, chloride, magnesium, pH, potassium, and sodium. Data-quality objectives were met by 78 percent of the samples analyzed for sulfate. Data-quality objectives were not met by samples analyzed for fluoride and specific conductance.

Introduction

The U.S. Geological Survey (USGS) maintains a laboratory at its Water Science Center in Troy, N.Y., to analyze low-ionic-strength water for USGS watershed-research projects that require major-ion analyses of precipitation, soil-water, shallow ground-water, and stream-water samples. The methods used in this laboratory are described in detail in Lawrence and others (1995). Quality-assurance and quality-control data were collected, stored, and reviewed through the laboratory's Lab Master information management system during this report period.

The 21 analytes represented by this study were: acid-neutralizing capacity (ANC), total monomeric aluminum, organic monomeric aluminum, total aluminum, ammonium, boron, calcium, dissolved organic carbon (DOC), chloride, fluoride, magnesium, nitrate (ion chromatograph), nitrite, total dissolved nitrogen, pH, potassium, silicon, sodium, specific conductance, sulfate, and turbidity.

Purpose and Scope

This report documents the quality-assurance practices and quality-control data of this laboratory and is intended for use by cooperating agencies. It (1) describes quality-control and quality-assurance procedures of the laboratory; (2) presents graphs showing the results from analyses of quality-control samples, filter blanks and analytical blanks, triplicate environmental samples, interlaboratory quality-assurance samples, and blind reference samples; and (3) describes analytical biases and outliers and the corrective actions taken.

Participating Projects

The numbers and types of samples analyzed by the laboratory during the 2-year period are summarized below, by the project for which they are associated.

Project: Neversink Watershed Study
Cooperator: New York City Department of Environmental Protection
Analyses: 12 samples (stream water, shallow ground water, and snow).

Project: Biogeochemical Processes that Control Nitrogen Cycling and Associated Hydrogen and Aluminum Leaching in an Undeveloped Headwater Basin
Cooperator: New York City Department of Environmental Protection
Analyses: 1,682 samples (stream water, shallow groundwater, soil-water solution, soil-water by expulsion method, and snow).

Project: Long-Term Monitoring of Five Streams in the Catskill Mountains
Cooperator: U.S. Environmental Protection Agency
Analyses: 642 stream-water samples.

Project: The Effects of the Clean Air Act on Water Quality of Medium-Scale Rivers in the Northeastern United States
Cooperator: U.S. Geological Survey, Office of Water Quality
Analysis: 258 stream-water samples.

Project: Adirondack Effects Assessment Program
Cooperator: Rensselaer Polytechnic Institute
Analyses: 702 stream-water samples.

Project: Upper and Lower Node Water-Quality Operation and Maintenance in the Catskill Mountains, New York
Cooperator: New York City Department of Environmental Protection
Analyses: 1,234 stream-water samples.

Project: Neversink River Natural Resources Study
Cooperator: The Nature Conservancy
Analysis: 98 stream-water samples.

Project: Collaborative Environmental Monitoring and Research Initiative
Cooperator: U.S. Geological Survey, Office of Water Quality and U.S. Forest Service
Analyses: 1,452 stream-water samples.

Project: Catskill Stream Restoration Study
Cooperator: New York City Department of Environmental Protection
Analyses: 98 stream-water samples.

Additional information on projects of the New York Water Science Center is given at *http://ny.water.usgs.gov.*

Quality-Assurance/Quality-Control (QA/QC) Program

The quality of the data produced at this laboratory is maintained by adherence to the standard operating procedures described in Lawrence and others (1995) and by participation in externally administered quality-assurance (QA) programs. Results of QA data are evaluated by the laboratory supervisor and primary analysts, and appropriate corrective action is taken when needed. The data-quality objectives (DQOs) are based on (1) the precision and accuracy levels generally required by projects that use the Troy Laboratory, and (2) the analytical limits of the methods used.

Quality-Control Samples

Quality-control (QC) samples are used to measure the accuracy of an instrument's calibration and to detect variations in instrument response within an analytical run. Source material for all QC samples either is obtained from a manufacturer other than the producer of the source material used to make calibration standards or is obtained from a lot other than the source material used to make calibration standards.

The concentrations of QC samples are chosen to bracket the expected range of the environmental sample concentrations. A high-concentration QC sample and a low-concentration QC sample (referred to herein as QC-high and QC-low respectively) are prepared for most analyses; exceptions are inorganic monomeric aluminum, for which column efficiency is used to determine the acceptability of the data; fluoride, for which only one mid-level QC sample is prepared because the concentrations encountered by the laboratory are within a narrow range; and turbidity, for which a second set of calibration standards is checked against the daily calibration response factor of the instrument.

QC-high and QC-low samples are analyzed within a run for most constituents; exceptions are ANC, pH, and specific conductance. Either the QC-high sample or the QC-low sample is analyzed within an ANC, pH, and specific conductance run, depending upon the expected concentration range of the environmental samples.

Quality-control samples are analyzed immediately after instrument calibration, after every 10 analyses of environmental samples, and at the end of each run. QC samples that do not meet DQOs for accuracy are rerun, and if the value is acceptable, the run is continued. If the rerun QC sample value is unacceptable, the environmental-sample data preceding it are considered to be out-of-control, the data are rejected, and the instrument is recalibrated. Only accepted QC-sample and environmental-sample data are entered into the database. An exception to this practice occurs when the volume of an environmental sample is insufficient for a rerun; in this case, the environmental sample and QC data are entered into the database and flagged, and the project chief then decides whether to use or exclude these data from the reports. The analytical results of QC samples in this report indicate (1) the frequency of out-of-control data that are not rerun, and (2) biases and trends of control data. The numbers of samples analyzed and a summary of the quality-assurance data are given in table 1.

Filter Blanks and Analytical Blanks

A filter blank and an analytical blank are included in each group of 50 environmental samples.

Filter blanks are aliquots of deionized (DI) water that are processed and analyzed in the same manner as environmental samples. Filter blanks are analyzed only for constituents that require filtration. Filter-blank analysis indicates whether contamination has occurred during any step in sample handling, including bottle-washing procedures, filtration, sample preservation, or laboratory analysis.

Analytical blanks are aliquots of DI water that are processed and analyzed as environmental samples, except that the filtration step is omitted. Contamination found in analytical blanks may be attributed to any step in sample-handling, but not to filtration.

Table 1. Number of environmental and quality-control (QC) samples analyzed by the USGS Laboratory in Troy, N.Y., and summary of quality-control data for each constituent, July 2001 through June 2003.

[QC-high, high-concentration quality-control sample; QC-low, low-concentration quality-control sample]

Constituent	Number of samples analyzed			Number of QC samples exceeding control limits where environmental sample data are not rejected		Number of QC samples exceeding control limits by more than 5 percent where environmental sample data are not rejected	
	Environmental samples	QC-high samples	QC-low samples	QC-high	QC-low	QC-high	QC-low
Acid-neutralizing capacity	5,837	528	234	19	5	0	0
Aluminum, total monomeric	6,126	676	674	1	1	0	0
Aluminum, organic monomeric[1]	6,126	0	0	0	0	0	0
Aluminum, total	6,853	957	959	0	0	0	0
Ammonium	5,888	764	765	3	1	0	0
Boron	443	36	36	0	0	0	0
Calcium	6,063	851	846	0	0	0	0
Carbon, dissolved organic	5,899	879	881	2	5	0	0
Chloride	6,093	809	823	0	3	0	0
Fluoride	1,681	0	200	0	3	0	0
Magnesium	6,064	851	846	0	0	0	0
Nitrate (ion chromatography)	6,086	809	823	1	12	0	0
Nitrite	4,052	512	512	5	5	0	0
Nitrogen, total dissolved	4,053	517	517	4	7	1	3
pH	6,044	615	284	18	6	0	0
Potassium	5,988	809	807	0	0	0	0
Silicon	6,064	848	841	0	0	0	0
Sodium	5,976	737	735	0	0	0	0
Specific conductance	6,010	584	222	0	5	0	1
Sulfate	6,083	809	823	1	5	0	0
Turbidity[2]	97	0	0	0	0	0	0

[1]Column efficiency is used to determine the acceptability of the data.

[2] Comparison of standards to calibration response factor is used to determine the acceptability of the data.

Triplicate Environmental Samples

One set of triplicate environmental samples is included in each group of 50 samples. An environmental triplicate set consists of three consecutive samples collected at one field site. The purpose of environmental triplicate samples is to determine long-term analytical precision. Precision can be affected by bottle washing, sample-collection or sample-processing procedures, and analysis. Environmental samples are selected for triplicate analysis on a random basis to ensure a wide range of sample concentrations from several field sites. The laboratory alternates between analyzing a triplicate set consecutively and separating the triplicate set over a day or multiple days of analytical runs.

U.S. Geological Survey's Standard Reference Sample Project

The USGS Standard Reference Sample (SRS) Project conducts a national interlaboratory analytical evaluation program semiannually. The Troy Laboratory participates in the low-ionic-strength, nutrient, and trace components of this program. Typically, the reference samples consist of snow, rain, surface water, or deionized water that is collected, filtered, and possibly spiked with reagent-grade chemicals to meet the goals of the program. Reference samples for low-ionic-strength constituents are prefixed by a P and are analyzed for calcium, chloride, fluoride, magnesium, pH, potassium, sodium, specific conductance, and sulfate. Reference samples for nutrient constituents are prefixed by an N and are analyzed for ammonium and nitrate. Reference samples for trace constituents are prefixed by a T and are analyzed for aluminum, calcium, magnesium, potassium, silicon, and sodium. Laboratory personnel are aware of the presence of the SRS sample at the time of analysis but do not know the constituent concentrations until a published report is received from the USGS after the conclusion of each study. The most probable value (MPV) for each constituent is equal to the median value calculated from the results submitted by participating laboratories. Laboratory performance is rated numerically by comparing analysis results to the MPVs for each constituent; the highest score is 4.0, and the lowest is 0.0.

National Water Research Institute Ecosystem Interlaboratory QA Program

The Troy Laboratory participates in Environment Canada's NWRI Ecosystem Interlaboratory QA program, in which a set of 10 samples is analyzed twice per year. The samples are obtained from predominantly low-ionic-strength waters from several sources, such as precipitation, snow, lakes, and streams throughout North America. The concentrations of the constituents in the NWRI samples are similar to those of the environmental samples analyzed at the Troy Laboratory. Laboratory results are compared with a median concentration value (MCV) calculated from results from all participants in the NWRI program. Laboratory personnel are aware of the presence of NWRI samples at the time of analysis but do not know the MCV of the constituents until Environment Canada publishes a report at the conclusion of each study.

Blind Reference Samples

The Troy Laboratory disguises USGS SRS samples from previous studies as routine environmental samples. These blind reference samples are processed and analyzed as environmental samples and therefore appear to the analyst to be project samples. The blind reference samples have MPVs that were reported by the USGS SRS project. The SRS samples are rotated as supplies are exhausted, and periodically the identity of the blind reference sample is changed. One blind reference sample is included in each set of 50 environmental samples. The Troy Laboratory used SRS P-samples as the blind reference samples during the time period represented in this report.

Control-Chart Evaluation

Control charts (figs. 1–5) are plots of QC data through time. This report uses control charts to (1) indicate whether the laboratory DQOs are met for individual QC samples, (2) reveal long-term biases within and outside the control limits, and (3) provide comparisons with results from other laboratories.

Each analyte has prescribed control limits that have been established to meet project DQOs (table 2). A constituent analysis is considered biased if 70 percent or more of the points on a chart are above or below the target value.

Quality-Control Samples

QC sample analysis data are plotted on control charts (fig. 1) in which the central line is equal to the target value of the control sample. The control limits for the samples are represented by the upper and lower control-limit lines on each chart. QC-high and QC-low samples are plotted on separate graphs by constituent and date of analysis, and the control charts are evaluated for trends and(or) bias and precision. All data are reported in micromoles per liter (μmol/L) except for pH (pH units), ANC (microequivalents per liter, μeq/L), and specific conductance (microsiemens per centimeter, μS/cm).

Filter Blanks and Analytical Blanks

Results from the blank analyses are plotted on control charts by constituent in figure 2. The control limits are represented by horizontal lines on the control charts. Data are plotted as concentration in relation to date of collection. Negative blank concentrations are encountered frequently. During analysis the instrument calibration curve is extrapolated beyond the lowest standard in order to evaluate blank samples, and negative concentrations reflect the practical limitations of the extrapolation. An outlier on the control chart indicates possible contamination.

Triplicate Environmental Samples

The coefficient of variation (CV) for each triplicate sample concentration is plotted by constituent and date of collection in figure 3. Data with mean concentrations less than the defined reporting limit (table 2) are excluded. The DQO for all constituents is a CV of less than 10 percent, with the exception of ANC, total monomeric aluminum, organic monomeric aluminum, total aluminum, and ammonium, for which the CV is 15 percent. Each circle within the control charts represents the CV of a triplicate environmental sample.

$$CV = \frac{s}{\overline{X}}(100) \tag{1}$$

where s =   standard deviation,
and $\overline{X}$ =   arithmetic mean of triplicate samples.

The ANC data are plotted on two graphs. The first (fig. 3A1) shows the CV for triplicate sample means outside the range of ±20 μeq/L; the absolute value of the mean is used to calculate the CV. The second (fig. 3A2) shows values within ±20 μeq/L; each symbol on the second graph represents the difference between the triplicate sample mean and the individual values of that triplicate sample.

Table 2. Reporting limits and data-quality objectives (DQOs) for accuracy, precision, and blanks for solution analyses performed by the USGS Laboratory in Troy, N.Y., July 2001 through June 2003.

[ANC, acid-neutralizing capacity; CV, coefficient of variation; DQO, data-quality objective; µmol/L, micromoles per liter; QC, quality control]

Constituent or property	Reporting limit (µmol/L)	Accuracy				Precision	
		Low-concentration QC sample		High-concentration QC sample		Environmental triplicate samples DQO (CV)	Filter and analytical blanks DQO (µmol/L)
		DQO (percent error)	Concentration (µmol/L)	DQO (percent error)	Concentration (µmol/L)		
Acid-neutralizing capacity[1]	none	10	(-39.9)	10	(125)	15	none
Aluminum, total monomeric	1.5	15	7.41	10	18.5	15	1.0
Aluminum, organic monomeric[2]	1.5	none	none	none	none	15	1.0
Aluminum, total	1.0	15	1.49	10	11.2	15	1.0
Ammonium	2.0	15	7.14	10	17.9	15	1.5
Boron	1.0	10	3.70	10	18.5	10	1.0
Calcium	2.0	10	25.0	10	99.8	10	1.0
Carbon, dissolved organic[3]	41.0	15	83.3	10	416	10	18
Chloride	3.0	10	8.47	10	84.7	10	2.0
Fluoride	0.5	20	1.58	none	none	10	0.6
Magnesium	1.0	10	10.3	10	41.1	10	0.5
Nitrate (ion chromatography)	2.0	10	4.84	10	48.4	10	0.3
Nitrite	0.5	15	7.14	10	28.6	10	1.0
Nitrogen, total dissolved	0.5	15	21.4	10	100	10	2.0
pH[4]	none	10	(4.44)	20	(6.88)	10	none
Potassium	1.0	10	6.40	10	25.6	10	0.5
Silicon	6.0	10	35.6	10	107	10	3.0
Sodium	1.0	10	10.9	10	43.5	10	1.0
Specific conductance[5]	none	15	(17.0)	15	(39.0)	10	1.5
Sulfate	2.0	10	8.33	10	83.3	10	0.3
Turbidity[6]	none	5	none	none	none	none	none

[1]ANC: values in parentheses are in microequivalents per liter. For values within ±20 microequivalents per liter, an absolute DQO of ±6 microequivalents per liter is used for precision.

[2]Quality-control samples for organic monomeric aluminum are unavailable.

[3]Concentrations are expressed as micromoles carbon per liter.

[4]pH: percent error and coefficient of variation are calculated from [H^+]. Values in parentheses are in pH units.

[5]Specific conductance: values in parentheses are in microsiemens per centimeter.

[6]Comparison standards must be within 5 percent of the daily response factor of the instrument.

National Water Research Institute Ecosystem Interlaboratory QA Program

Interlaboratory-comparison graphs (fig. 4) are based on results from NWRI samples and represent NWRI studies from September 1999 through April 2001. Sample data with MCVs less than the Troy Laboratory reporting limits were excluded. The MCV and the control limits are represented by lines on the graphs; the percent difference (D) is calculated as:

$$D = \frac{AV - MCV}{MCV} \times 100 \qquad (2)$$

where AV =   analyzed value,

and MCV =   mean concentration value.

A separate graph is shown for ANC values within the ±20-µeq/L range (fig. 4A2); these results are plotted as the difference between the laboratory value and the MCV. The pH results consist of two sets of data—values less than 6.00, and values equal to or greater than 6.00. The two sets of data have different DQOs, which are represented by a short dashed line and a long dashed line on the pH graph (fig. 4I).

Blind Reference Samples

Results from blind reference sample analyses are plotted in figure 5 by constituent and date of analysis. Sample data with MPVs less than the reporting limits were excluded. The MPV and the control limits of ±10 percent are represented by lines on the graphs; the percent difference (D) is calculated as

$$D = \frac{AV - MPV}{MPV} \times 100 \qquad (3)$$

where AV =   analyzed value,

and MPV =   most probable value.

Summary of Results

The following sections summarize the results for (A) quality-control samples (fig. 1), (B) filter blanks and analytical blanks (fig. 2), (C) triplicate environmental samples (fig. 3), (D) SRS samples (table 3), (E) NWRI samples (fig. 4), and (F) blind samples (fig. 5).

A. Quality-Control Samples

Acid-Neutralizing Capacity (fig. 1A).— DQOs were met by 98 percent of the samples. The QC-high sample had a negative bias from September 2002 through June 2003. The QC-low sample had a positive bias in 2002.

Aluminum, Total Monomeric (fig. 1B).—DQOs were met by 99 percent of the samples. No apparent trends or biases were evident for the QC-high sample. The QC-low sample had a positive bias during this period.

Aluminum, Total (fig. 1C).—DQOs were met by 100 percent of the samples. The QC-high sample and the QC-low sample had a positive bias during this period.

Ammonium (fig. 1D).—DQOs were met by 99 percent of the samples. No apparent trends or biases were evident during this period.

Boron (fig. 1E).—DQOs were met by 100 percent of the samples. There are insufficient data to establish any apparent trends or biases during this period.

Calcium (fig. 1F).—DQOs were met by 100 percent of the samples. The QC-high sample had a slight positive bias during this period. No apparent trends or biases were evident for the QC-low sample.

Carbon, Dissolved Organic (fig. 1G).—DQOs were met by 99 percent of the samples. No apparent trends or biases were evident during this period.

Chloride (fig. 1H).—DQOs were met by 99 percent of the samples. The QC-high sample had a positive bias in 2001 and 2003; the remaining time it indicated a slight negative bias. No apparent trends or biases were evident for the QC-low sample.

Fluoride (fig. 1I).—DQOs were met by 98 percent of the samples. The QC sample had a positive bias during this period.

Magnesium (fig. 1J).—DQOs were met by 100 percent of the samples. The QC-high sample had a positive bias through 2001. The QC-low sample had a negative bias during this period.

Nitrate (ion chromatography) (fig. 1K).—DQOs were met by 99 percent of the samples. The QC-high sample had a positive bias in 2001 and 2003. No apparent trends or biases were evident for the QC-low sample.

Nitrite (fig. 1L).—DQOs were met by 99 percent of the samples. No apparent trends or biases were evident during this period.

Nitrogen, Total Dissolved (fig. 1M).—DQOs were met by 99 percent of the samples. No apparent trends or biases were evident during this period.

pH (fig. 1N).—DQOs were met by 97 percent of the samples. The QC-high sample had a negative bias through June 2002. The QC-low sample had a positive bias during this period.

Potassium (fig. 1O).—DQOs were met by 100 percent of the samples. The QC-high sample and the QC-low sample had a positive bias through August 2002.

Silicon (fig. 1P).—DQOs were met by 100 percent of the samples. No apparent trends or biases were evident during this period.

Sodium (fig. 1Q).—DQOs were met by 100 percent of the samples. The QC-high sample had a negative bias through February 2002 and in May 2003. The QC-low sample had a negative bias during this period.

Specific Conductance (fig. 1R).—DQOs were met by 99 percent of the samples. The QC-high sample and the QC-low sample had a negative bias during this period.

Sulfate (fig. 1S).—DQOs were met by 99 percent of the samples. The QC-high sample had a positive bias during this period. The QC-low sample had a positive bias through 2002.

B. Filter Blanks and Analytical Blanks

Aluminum, Total Monomeric (fig. 2A).—The DQO was met by 100 percent of the samples. No systematic trends were evident for this analysis.

Aluminum, Organic Monomeric (fig. 2B).—The DQO was met by 100 percent of the samples. No systematic trends were evident for this analysis.

Aluminum, Total.—(fig. 2C).—The DQO was met for 96 percent of the samples. No systematic trends were evident for this analysis.

Ammonium.—(fig. 2D).—The DQO was met by 84 percent of the samples. Blank data results show improvement in December 2002 through 2003 when 99 percent of the samples met the DQO.

Boron (fig. 2E).—The DQO was met by 100 percent of the samples. There are insufficient data for trend analysis.

Calcium (fig. 2F).—The DQO was met by 92 percent of the samples. No systematic trends were evident for this analysis.

Carbon, Dissolved Organic (fig. 2G).—The DQO was not met for DOC. Blank data results are significantly higher in DOC concentrations since a new instrument was purchased in 1998. The current DQO and the instrument operating procedures are being evaluated.

Chloride (fig. 2H).—The DQO was met by 72 percent of the samples. Chloride contamination peaked in late 2002 when the laboratory was experiencing deionized water tank quality issues.

Fluoride (fig. 2I).—The DQO was met by 99 percent of the samples. Fluoride blank values increased in 2002 and remained higher during 2003.

Magnesium (fig. 2J).—The DQO was met by 99 percent of the samples. No systematic trends were evident for this analysis.

Nitrate (ion chromatography) (fig. 2K).—The DQO was met by 99 percent of the samples. No systematic trends were evident for this analysis.

Nitrite (fig. 2L).—The DQO was met by 100 percent of the samples. No systematic trends were evident for this analysis.

Nitrogen, Total Dissolved (fig. 2M).— The DQO was met by 86 percent of the samples. No systematic trends were evident for this analysis.

Potassium (fig. 2N).—The DQO was met by 80 percent of the samples. Potassium blank values peaked in late 2002 when the laboratory was experiencing deionized water tank quality issues.

Silicon (fig. 2O).—The DQO was met by 82 percent of the samples. Silicon blank values peaked in late 2002 when the laboratory was experiencing deionized water tank quality issues.

Sodium (fig. 2P).—The DQO was met by 80 percent of the samples. Sodium blank values peaked in late 2002 when the laboratory was experiencing deionized water tank quality issues.

Specific Conductance (fig. 2Q).—The DQO was not met for specific conductance. Specific conductance blank values peaked in late 2002 when the laboratory was experiencing deionized water tank quality issues. The DQO was met by 92 percent of the samples for the remainder of the period.

Sulfate (fig. 2R).—The DQO was met by 99 percent of the samples. No systematic trends were evident for this analysis.

C. Triplicate Environmental Samples

Acid-Neutralizing Capacity (figs. 3A1 and 3A2).—The DQO was met by 96 percent of the triplicate samples.

Aluminum, Total Monomeric (fig. 3B).—The DQO was met by 83 percent of the triplicate samples.

Aluminum, Organic Monomeric (fig. 3C).—The DQO was met by 100 percent of the triplicate samples.

Aluminum, Total (fig. 3D).—The DQO was met by 76 percent of the triplicate samples.

Ammonium (fig. 3E).—The DQO was met by 73 percent of the triplicate samples.

Boron.— There were insufficient boron triplicate data to create a control chart.

Calcium (fig. 3F).—The DQO was met by 96 percent of the triplicate samples.

Carbon, Dissolved Organic (fig. 3G).—The DQO was met by 86 percent of the triplicate samples.

Chloride (fig. 3H).—The DQO was met by 91 percent of the triplicate samples.

Fluoride (fig. 3I).—The DQO was met by 97 percent of the triplicate samples.

Magnesium (fig. 3J).—The DQO was met by 97 percent of the triplicate samples.

Nitrate (ion chromatography) (fig. 3K).—The DQO was met by 81 percent of the triplicate samples.

Nitrite.— There were insufficient nitrite triplicate data to create a control chart.

Nitrogen, Total Dissolved (fig. 3L).—The DQO was met by 56 percent of the triplicate samples.

pH (fig. 3M).—The DQO was met by 99 percent of the triplicate samples.

Potassium (fig. 3N).—The DQO was met by 90 percent of the triplicate samples.

Silicon (fig. 3O).—The DQO was met by 100 percent of the triplicate samples.

Sodium (fig. 3P).—The DQO was met by 92 percent of the triplicate samples.

Specific Conductance (fig. 3Q).—The DQO was met by 93 percent of the triplicate samples.

Sulfate (fig. 3R).—The DQO was met by 93 percent of the triplicate samples.

D. U.S. Geological Survey's Standard Reference Sample Project

The USGS SRS Project rates laboratory performance for each analyte on a scale of 4 to 0:

Rating	Performance
4.0	Excellent
3.0–3.99	Good
2.0–2.99	Satisfactory
1.0–1.99	Marginal
0.0–0.99	Unsatisfactory

Missing SRS results for the Troy Laboratory were due to instrument downtime during the SRS study period.

All analyses (table 3) received a satisfactory or better rating for each constituent with the following exceptions:

Ammonium.—The zero rating for SRS N–71 was for a result very close to the laboratory's ammonium reporting limit.

Magnesium.—The zero rating for SRS T–169 was for a value which was 12 percent above the SRS most probable value.

Potassium.—The rating of 1 for SRS T–169 was for a value which was 8 percent above the SRS most probable value.

Sodium.—The cause of a zero rating for SRS T–173 was an erroneous dilution calculation. The laboratory was sent an additional sample for this study which received a rating of 4.

Table 3. Results obtained by the USGS Laboratory in Troy, N.Y., for the U.S. Geological Survey Standard Reference Sample (SRS) Project, September 2001 through March 2003.

[MPV, most probable value; TV, Troy Laboratory value. All values are in milligrams per liter except aluminum (micrograms per liter, μg/L), pH (pH units), and specific conductance (microsiemens per centimeter, μS/cm). Dashes indicate no results reported]

Analyte	MPV, TV, and rating[a]	SRS sample number and date of sample distribution											
		T–167 09–01[b]	N–71 09–01[b]	P–37 09–01[b]	T–169 03–02[c]	N–73 03–02[c]	P–38 03–02[c]	T–171 09–02[d]	N–75 09–02[d]	P–39 09–02[d]	T–173 03–03[e]	N–77 03–03[e]	P–40 03–03[e]
Aluminum	MPV	21.5	—	—	33.6	—	—	19.4	—	—	71	—	—
	TV	20.5	—	—	34.1	—	—	18.6	—	—	71.7	—	—
	Rating	4	—	—	4	—	—	4	—	—	4	—	—
Ammonium[f]	MPV	—	0.063	—	—	0.127	—	—	0.077	—	—	0.073	—
	TV	—	0.041	—	—	0.139	—	—	0.09	—	—	0.08	—
	Rating	—	0	—	—	2	—	—	2	—	—	3	—
Calcium	MPV	5.15	—	1.03	37.6	—	6.4	6.75	—	8.65	34.8	—	0.728
	TV	5.09	—	1	36.6	—	6.4	6.82	—	8.46	34.9	—	0.756
	Rating	4	—	4	3	—	4	4	—	4	4	—	3
Chloride	MPV	—	—	3.1	—	—	8.37	—	—	2.07	—	—	15.2
	TV	—	—	3.26	—	—	8.17	—	—	1.98	—	—	14.9
	Rating	—	—	3	—	—	4	—	—	3	—	—	4
Fluoride	MPV	—	—	—	—	—	—	—	—	—	—	—	0.127
	TV	—	—	—	—	—	—	—	—	—	—	—	0.124
	Rating	—	—	—	—	—	—	—	—	—	—	—	4
Magnesium	MPV	4.8	—	0.506	4.3	—	1.15	2.78	—	0.812	9.38	—	1.62
	TV	4.56	—	0.477	4.83	—	1.11	2.8	—	0.758	9.29	—	1.57
	Rating	3	—	3	0	—	3	4	—	2	4	—	4
Nitrate	MPV	—	0.067	—	—	—	—	—	0.092	—	—	0.067	—
	TV	—	0.061	—	—	—	—	—	0.09	—	—	0.068	—
	Rating	—	2	—	—	—	—	—	4	—	—	4	—
pH	MPV	—	—	4.61	—	—	6.01	—	—	3.66	—	—	—
	TV	—	—	4.61	—	—	5.94	—	—	3.68	—	—	—
	Rating	—	—	4	—	—	4	—	—	4	—	—	—
Potassium	MPV	4.76	—	0.5	2.59	—	0.83	—	—	—	3.85	—	0.384
	TV	4.93	—	0.5	2.79	—	0.839	—	—	—	3.68	—	0.357
	Rating	3	—	4	1	—	4	—	—	—	3	—	3
Silicon[g]	MPV	5.9	—	—	6.04	—	—	3.5	—	—	11.1	—	—
	TV	5.76	—	—	6.05	—	—	3.49	—	—	11	—	—
	Rating	4	—	—	4	—	—	4	—	—	4	—	—
Sodium	MPV	7.34	—	0.8	10.6	—	1.8	—	—	—	36.5	—	5.42
	TV	7.18	—	0.777	10.1	—	1.77	—	—	—	64.4	—	5.08
	Rating	4	—	4	3	—	4	—	—	—	0	—	2
Specific conductance	MPV	—	—	28.3	—	—	65	—	—	193	—	—	66.8
	TV	—	—	27.7	—	—	61.5	—	—	183	—	—	63.3
	Rating	—	—	4	—	—	2	—	—	2	—	—	2
Sulfate	MPV	—	—	1.44	—	—	2.99	—	—	29.3	—	—	0.89
	TV	—	—	1.44	—	—	3.01	—	—	28.2	—	—	0.865
	Rating	—	—	4	—	—	4	—	—	3	—	—	4

[a]Laboratory rating system: 4 is highest score; 0 is lowest.   [b]Sample described in Woodworth and Connor (2001).
[c]Sample described in Woodworth and Connor (2002).   [d]Sample described in Woodworth and Connor (2003a).
[e]Sample described in Woodworth and Connor (2003b).   [f]The SRS Project reports data as "Ammonia as Nitrogen."
[g]The SRS Project reports data as "Silica."

E. National Water Resource Institute Ecosystem Interlaboratory QA Program

Environment Canada's NWRI program does not audit the analysis of total monomeric aluminum, organic monomeric aluminum, boron, fluoride, nitrite, total dissolved nitrogen, and turbidity.

Acid-Neutralizing Capacity (figs. 4A1 and 4A2).—The DQO was met by 63 percent of the NWRI samples. Data outliers exhibited a negative bias except for study 82 which had a positive bias.

Aluminum, Total (fig. 4B).—The DQO was met by 94 percent of the NWRI samples. The data exhibited a positive bias except for study 81.

Ammonium (fig. 4C).—The DQO was not met for the NWRI samples. The reporting limit for ammonium is being reevaluated.

Calcium (fig. 4D).—The DQO was met by 98 percent of the NWRI samples. No trend or bias was evident.

Carbon, Dissolved Organic (fig. 4E).—The DQO was met by 72 percent of the NWRI samples. The data outliers exhibited a positive bias.

Chloride (fig. 4F).—The DQO was met by 90 percent of the NWRI samples. The data outliers exhibited a positive bias; the data exhibited a negative bias during studies 81 and 82.

Magnesium (fig. 4G).—The DQO was met by 100 percent of the NWRI samples. The data exhibited a slight negative bias.

Nitrate (ion chromatography) (fig. 4H).—The DQO was met by 100 percent of the NWRI samples. The data exhibited a positive bias except for study 81.

pH (fig. 4I).—The DQO was met by 100 percent of the NWRI samples. The data exhibited a negative bias.

Potassium (fig. 4J).—The DQO was met by 90 percent of the NWRI samples. Data outliers exhibited a positive bias except for study 82 which had a negative bias.

Silicon (fig. 4K).—The DQO was met by 100 percent of the NWRI samples. The data exhibited a negative bias.

Sodium (fig. 4L).—The DQO was met by 70 percent of the NWRI samples. The data exhibited a negative bias for studies 79 and 82 and a positive bias for studies 80 and 81.

Specific Conductance (fig. 4M).—The DQO was met by 90 percent of the NWRI samples. The data exhibited a negative bias.

Sulfate (fig. 4N).—The DQO was met by 95 percent of the NWRI samples. The data exhibited a slight negative bias for studies 80 through 82.

F. Blind Reference Samples

Blind reference samples (SRS low-ionic-strength constituent P-samples) are analyzed for the Troy Laboratory procedures for which the SRS project reports an analyte MPV. The blind reference samples are not analyzed for acid-neutralizing capacity, total monomeric aluminum, organic monomeric aluminum, total aluminum, ammonium, boron, dissolved organic carbon, nitrate, nitrite, total dissolved nitrogen, silicon, and turbidity.

Calcium (fig. 5A).—The DQO for calcium was met by 98 percent of the blind reference samples. The data exhibited a negative bias for this period.

Chloride (fig. 5B).—The DQO was met by 90 percent of the blind reference samples. A positive bias was evident in 2003.

Fluoride (fig. 5C).—The DQO was not met. Since the laboratory has a history of good fluoride results, it is possible that the fluoride most probable value is unstable for the blind samples used during the latter part of the period.

Magnesium (fig. 5D).—The DQO was met by 90 percent of the blind reference samples. Data indicated a negative bias.

pH (fig. 5E).—The DQO was met by 91 percent of the blind reference samples. A positive bias was evident.

Potassium (fig. 5F).—The DQO was met by 92 percent of the blind reference samples. A negative bias was evident in 2003.

Sodium (fig. 5G).—The DQO was met by 91 percent of the blind reference samples. Data indicated a negative bias.

Specific Conductance (fig. 5H).—The DQO was not met. The blind sample used in 2001 is listed as an unstable value on the SRS project web site.

Sulfate (fig. 5I).—The DQO was met by 78 percent of the samples. Data indicated a negative bias.

Selected References

Lawrence, G.B., Lincoln, T.A., Horan-Ross, D.A., Olson, M.L., and Waldron, L.A., 1995, Analytical methods of the U.S. Geological Survey's New York District Water Analysis Laboratory: U.S. Geological Survey Open-File Report 95–416, 78 p.

Lincoln, T.A., Horan-Ross, D.A., McHale, M.R., and Lawrence, G.B., 2001, Quality-assurance data for routine water analyses by the U.S. Geological Survey Laboratory in Troy, New York—July 1993 through June 1995: U.S. Geological Survey Open-File Report 01–171, 25 p.

Lincoln, T.A., Horan-Ross, D.A., McHale, M.R., and Lawrence, G.B., 2004, Quality-assurance data for routine water analyses by the U.S. Geological Survey Laboratory in Troy, New York—July 1995 through June 1997: U.S. Geological Survey Open-File Report 2004–1327, 25 p.

Lincoln, T.A., Horan-Ross, D.A., McHale, M.R., and Lawrence, G.B., 2006, Quality-assurance data for routine water analyses by the U.S. Geological Survey Laboratory in Troy, New York—July 1997 through June 1999: U.S. Geological Survey Open-File Report 2006–1245, 25 p.

Lincoln, T.A., Horan-Ross, D.A., McHale, M.R., and Lawrence, G.B., 2006, Quality-assurance data for routine water analyses by the U.S. Geological Survey Laboratory in Troy, New York—July 1999 through June 2001: U.S. Geological Survey Open-File Report 2006–1246, 27 p.

Lincoln, T.A., Horan-Ross, D.A., Olson, M.L., and Lawrence, G.B., 1996, Quality-assurance data for routine water analyses by the U.S. Geological Survey Laboratory in Troy, New York—May 1991 through June 1993: U.S. Geological Survey Open-File Report 96–167, 22 p.

Woodworth, M.T., and Connor, B.F., 2001, Results of the U.S. Geological Survey's analytical evaluation program for standard reference samples distributed in September 2001: U.S. Geological Survey Open-File Report 02–8, 113 p.

Woodworth, M.T., and Connor, B.F., 2002, Results of the U.S. Geological Survey's analytical evaluation program for standard reference samples distributed in March 2002: U.S. Geological Survey Open-File Report 02–243, 108 p.

Woodworth, M.T., and Connor, B.F., 2003a, Results of the U.S. Geological Survey's analytical evaluation program for standard reference samples distributed in September 2002: U.S. Geological Survey Open-File Report 02–481, 108 p.

Woodworth, M.T., and Connor, B.F., 2003b, Results of the U.S. Geological Survey's analytical evaluation program for standard reference samples distributed in March 2003: U.S. Geological Survey Open-File Report 03–261, 109 p.

Figures 1–5

For more information concerning this report, contact

Director
U.S. Geological Survey
New York Water Science Center
425 Jordan Road
Troy, NY 12180-8349
dc_ny@usgs.gov

or visit our Web site at:
http://ny.water.usgs.gov

Lincoln and others—Quality-Assurance Data for Routine Water Analyses by the Laboratory in Troy, New York—July 2001 through June 2003—Open-File Report 2009-1232

USGS

www.ingramcontent.com/pod-product-compliance
Lightning Source LLC
Chambersburg PA
CBHW080349290526
45791CB00009BA/2798